Painting Animals on Rocks

on Rocks

Tips & Techniques for Fabulous Fun

Illustrated by **Raffaella & Jessica Dowling**

Photography by **F. William Lagaret**

Text by **Jessica Dowling**

Mud Puddle
NEW YORK

W9-ARS-377

Painting Animals on Rocks:
Tips & Techniques for Fabulous Fun
Illustrated by Raffaella and Jessica Dowling
Photography by F. William Lagaret
Text by Jessica Dowling

© 2008 by Mud Puddle Books, Inc.

Published by
Mud Puddle, Inc.
36 W. 25th Street
New York, NY 10010
info@mudpuddleinc.com

ISBN: 978-1-60311-182-9

Printed in China

Contents

Why Paint Rocks?

Rock painting is an easy and inexpensive way to create your own art! Painting rocks allows you to use your creativity in ways different than when you paint on paper or canvas. By studying the shape of the rock you can imagine all sorts of things that the rock could become.

What can I do with painted rocks?

Painted rocks make unique and expressive indoor or outdoor decorations. Put them on your mantle, your nightstand, or even use larger ones for bookends. They are great patio decorations, and a few tucked

in a flowerpot always look pretty. Don't forget: painted rocks make wonderful gifts, too!

don't know how to paint!

Rock painting is the perfect medium for beginners. If you mess up, just prime the rock over again and start out fresh. In addition, since the shape of the rock often suggests a form, it is easier for the beginning artist to pick a subject. Painting rocks is great for advanced artists, too! Challenge yourself and see how detailed your rocks can become. When someone mistakenly bites into a rock you've painted to look like a cookie, you're an expert!

What do I paint on a rock?

Anything! Paint your favorite animal or flower, or create a rock with a sports theme. Paint a letter on each of several rocks, and spell out your name or that of a friend. Paint vegetables or fruits on rocks to

decorate a kitchen, or different sea creatures to decorate a bathroom. An apple-painted rock given to a teacher will last much longer than the real thing! The possibilities of what to paint are absolutely endless. Use your imagination!

Where can I find rocks?

Most arts and crafts stores sell smooth polished river stones. These have mostly round or oblong shapes; so if you want to find more unique rocks, get outside! Many rocks of varying shapes, sizes and textures can be found at the beach, or near rivers and lakes. If you live in a city, you can try looking for rocks in a park. Always make sure to have an adult with you when you go out looking for rocks.

Priming

Because rocks are often dark or bumpy, it is important to prime them before you paint your design. This prepares the rock to be painted on. To prime a rock, simply cover it with a thick coat of white paint and allow it to dry completely. It's okay if the rock's color still shows through; it will get covered up when you paint your design.

Materials

Acrylic Paint. A good basic set of paints would consist of white, black, red, blue, and yellow. You can mix most other colors you might want to use from these. You may, however, wish to invest in some extra paints since colors such as magenta and brown may be difficult to mix on your own. You'll find two-ounce bottles of acrylic craft paint are fairly inexpensive. They work great and cost much less than fine arts acrylics.

Acrylic brushes in several sizes. Consider starting out with a size 6 filbert, a size 4 round, and a size 0 round (for fine details). Try out different brush sizes as you determine your artistic needs.

Clear acrylic glaze to protect rocks that are displayed outside or to give your indoor rocks a brilliant sheen. This glaze comes in aerosol cans or in liquid form to be painted on. Use the liquid form for painting rocks because it adheres better, and you can apply it indoors. A small bottle (around 120 ml) should last a long time.

Toothpicks. These are great for painting tiny details or dots.

A cup of water to clean brushes.

Paper towels for surface cleanup.

Newspaper to lay on top of your work area and protect surfaces.

A pencil to sketch out your design on the rock. A soft pencil works best, as it will show up on the rock better. Instead of a standard #2 pencil, pick up a soft 6B pencil at an art supply store.

Scrap paper to jot down ideas. Always keep some paper with you in case a great idea for a painted rock strikes you when you are on the go!

Cat Rocks

TIP!

If rocks are dirty or muddy, wash them with warm water and dish soap, then pat dry with paper towels.

Puppy Rocks

If you'd like, sketch a loose design on a primed rock with a soft pencil before you start painting.

Pawprint Rocks

Don't leave brushes in your cup of water! This can cause the bristles and handle of your brush to get ruined. After washing your brushes, lay them on some paper towels to dry until you need them again. Well cared for brushes can last years

TIP!

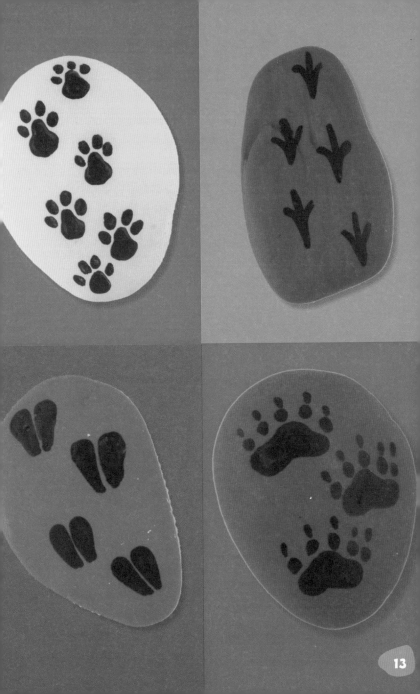

Bird
Rocks

TIP!

Make sure to take a break from painting every so often to give your hands and eyes a rest.

Bug Rocks

A little paint goes a long way! Put only a dab of each color on your palette, you can always add more.

TIP!

Frog Rocks

TIP!

The colors of your design will be clearer and more vibrant if you do a good job priming the rock first.

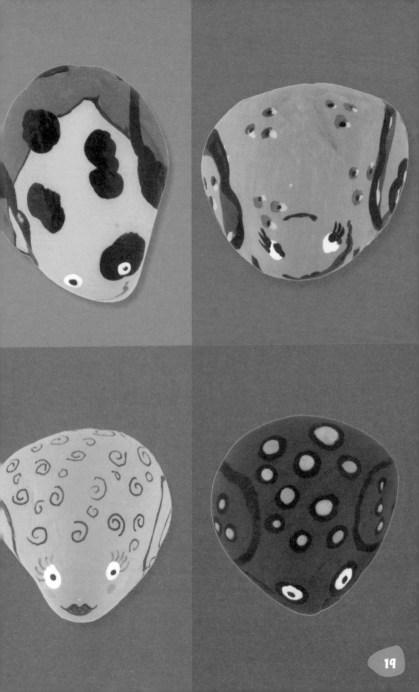

Wood Critters

TIP!

Use two or more painted rocks to create a composition. For instance, a rock with a tree painted on it, one with a bench, and one with a fountain make an adorable park!

Barnyard Rocks

Try to think of creative backgrounds for your subject matter. Don't always use white! Try bright colors, stripes, or even polka dots as a backdrop for your creations.

TIP!

23

Jungle Rocks

TIP!

To make rocks more brilliant, give them a coat of clear acrylic after they are completely dry.

Zoo Rocks

Experiment using a thin permanent marker on finished, totally dry rocks. Use it to outline objects, or add fine details.

TIP!

Ocean Rocks

TIP!

Change the water you use to clean your brushes often to prevent muddy colors.

Myth Rocks

TIP!

Painted rocks make great paperweights or doorstoppers!

I ♥ Painted Rocks!